The Ruth Heller Connection

by Will C. Howell

FEARON TEACHER AIDS
Simon & Schuster Supplementary Education Group

Ruth Heller,

Thank you for color. Thank you for playing with color and words and information and for turning it all into a wonderful discovery of the world that surrounds us. Thank you for supporting my effort to extend your books into continued discovery in the classroom.

Will Howell

Editor: Carol Williams
Copyeditor: Kristin Eclov
Illustration: Gwen Connelly
Cover illustration: Reprinted from *Merry-Go-Round* with the permission of
    Ruth Heller.
Design: Diann Abbott

ISBN 0-8224-1635-2

Printed in the United States of America
1. 9 8 7 6 5 4 3 2 1

Contents

Introduction

The emphasis on "The Year of the Young Reader" (1989), "International Literacy Year" (1990), and "The Year of the Lifetime Reader" (1991) has helped children's literature come of age. Research confirms that good reading and writing are best taught by using good books. And today, educators are fortunate to have a wide selection of excellent children's books to choose from.

The Ruth Heller Connection is written for librarians and teachers who want to effectively use good literature in their classrooms. The lessons present art, math, creative writing, science, and social studies activities to accompany books by this one outstanding author/illustrator. The variety of interdisciplinary activities and the whole-language instructional approach incorporated in the lessons will help you meet the diverse needs and interests of your students.

As students become familiar with various works by a single author/illustrator, they develop an ability to analyze literary and artistic style. Children can go to the library and select books written or illustrated by authors they feel as if they have actually met. "Connecting" with authors stimulates students to become involved in and enthusiastic about reading, writing, and learning. *The Ruth Heller Connection* gives students the opportunity to meet the author of *Chickens Aren't the Only Ones, A Cache of Jewels,* and other such colorful books about words and ideas.

Lessons require minimal preparation, while resulting in maximum participation and learning. A brief synopsis of each book is included. Read the book aloud to the children and invite them to enjoy the illustrations before participating in the activities. Exciting activities, including Vigorous Verbs, Pyramid Math, and Paper-Plate Merry-Go-Round, will help you to enhance and reinforce your curriculum.

Meet Ruth Heller

Ruth Heller was born on April 2, 1923.

Ms. Heller is the mother of two and lives with her husband in San Francisco, California. Besides working full-time writing books for children, she enjoys reading, cooking, going out to eat, playing tennis, going to the movies, and being with people. Ruth Heller's love of words and living permeates her work.

As a graphic artist, Ruth Heller began designing coloring books. As a result of research she was doing at the aquarium for a coloring book on tropical fish, Ruth Heller got an idea for her first children's book. *Chickens Aren't the Only Ones,* a book about birds, fish, and other creatures that lay eggs, was first met with rejection by many publishers. Ms. Heller persisted, revised her book, and was finally published. *Chickens Aren't the Only Ones* was chosen as a Children's Science Book Award Honor Book by the New York Academy of Sciences.

Once Ruth Heller gets an idea for a book, she begins the research. Then she outlines her book. Many sketches follow before she does the final art. Throughout the whole process, Ms. Heller is constantly revising the words. Finally, about a year later, she takes her completed manuscript to the publisher.

For her exquisite art work, Ruth Heller uses a variety of mediums. She usually begins by outlining in pen. Then she adds color with markers. After this, she uses prisma colors (oil-based pencils) for detailed coloring. She sometimes draws on colored paper as in *Chickens Aren't the Only Ones.* Other times, she might use a watercolor background as in *The Egyptian Cinderella.* The final product is a finely detailed, boldly colored book to be enjoyed by all ages.

Plants That Never Ever Bloom is one of Ruth Heller's favorites. Her curiosity and wonder for life are gifts that she shares in all her books. Students will find new ways to bloom and grow in their own lives as they delve into Ruth Heller's beautiful book collection.

Animals Born

With striking illustrations, Ruth Heller identifies a wide variety of mammals, from the tiny shrew to the huge blue whale. The witty and whimsical text highlights mammal characteristics.

New York: Grosset & Dunlap, 1982

Alive and Well

ELEPHANT CHAINS

Materials:

- worksheet on page 9
- scissors
- pencils
- crayons or markers
- clear tape
- encyclopedias and reference books (optional)

Lesson Procedure

1. Have students cut their worksheets apart on the dotted line, then fold each strip accordian-style into fourths.
2. Instruct students to cut around the elephant, being careful not to cut through any folded edges.
3. If cut correctly, students will have identical elephants linked together like paper dolls.
4. Give students the choice of writing a short story or poem or researching several facts to copy on the lined elephants.
5. Invite students to complete the unlined elephants by adding details, such as ears, eyes, mouth, and toes.
6. Using clear tape, connect the students' elephants, trunk to tail, to make a class elephant chain.

Taking It Further . . .

Encourage students to fold a piece of drawing paper into fourths, accordion-style, and design a new mammal chain. Remind students to think symmetrically.

Animals Born Alive and Well

• THE HOLE BOOK OF MAMMALS •

Materials:

- worksheet on page 11
- lined paper
- pencils
- encyclopedias and reference books
- scissors

Lesson Procedure

1. Instruct students to draw a mammal on the worksheet, using the hole as a part of the picture (an eye, an ear, a rock, or the end of a log). Remind students that the hole will be cut out of the picture. Anything that they draw on the hole will not be part of the picture.
2. Have students cut out the holes.
3. After they have completed their pictures, encourage students to use reference books to write 3 to 5 interesting facts about their mammals. Encourage students to write complete sentences on lined paper and edit the sentences before copying them on the worksheet.
4. Bind all the student pages together, lining up the holes, to make a class booklet.

Taking It Further . . .

Invite students to color their pictures with crayons or markers and add environmental detail with pieces of construction paper, tissue paper, or fabric.

Animals Born Alive and Well

Name _____

Cut out
hole.

_____

_____

_____

_____

_____

_____

The Ruth Heller Connection © 1992 Fearon Teacher Aids

MAMMAL MURAL

Materials:

- butcher paper
- construction paper
- pencils
- crayons or markers
- stapler
- glue
- scissors
- masking tape

Lesson Procedure

1. After reading *Animals Born Alive and Well,* show children the beautiful illustrations again. Ask students to identify the mammals. Point out the variety of environments in which mammals can live (jungle, desert, underground, ocean).
2. Divide the class into groups, with each group representing a different environment.
3. Invite each group to create a mural scene complete with background, foreground, and wandering mammals in the middle. The background should include physical features of the environment, such as mountains, and the foreground should include plant life.
4. Encourage students to make the mammals as accurately proportioned as possible out of construction paper. Attach the animals in place on the mural with a stapler or masking tape.

Taking It Further . . .

Use the mural as a learning tool. Carefully remove the mammals from the mural and ask students to place them in the correct environment. Or, place the animals incorrectly on the mural before students arrive one morning and ask them to identify the misplaced mammals.

❦ • THE SHAPES OF MAMMALS • ❧

Materials:

•mammal prints

Lesson Procedure

1. Divide the class into cooperative learning groups of 4 to 6 students.
2. Give each group of students 10 to 12 mammal prints.
3. Review with the students the attributes of several geometric shapes (circle, rectangle, and triangle). Draw a circle, triangle, and rectangle on the chalkboard for reference.
4. Invite students to categorize their mammal prints into groups according to the basic shape of each mammal. Remind students that there is no right or wrong way to categorize. The purpose of the activity is to identify shapes in nature. For example, a pig might look most like a circle and a giraffe like a triangle.

Taking It Further . . .

Give students drawing paper and challenge them to draw some mammals, beginning with basic geometric shapes.

❧ • LIONS AND LINES • ☙

Materials:

•mammal prints

Lesson Procedure

1. Discuss the different types of lines with the students. On the chalkboard, encourage students to draw examples of curved lines, straight lines, closed lines, open lines, parallel lines, and branching lines.
2. Divide the class into cooperative learning groups of 4 to 6 students.
3. Give each group of students 10 to 12 mammal prints. Ask the students to look for examples of different kinds of lines. Students may find a curved line on a camel's back, open lines for a porcupine's quills, parallel lines as a zebra's stripes, and branching lines as a deer's antlers.

Taking It Further . . .

Challenge students to use different kinds of lines to draw several different mammals.

A Cache of

Ruth Heller presents readers with a fascinating look at a bundle of collective nouns lavishly illustrated in bold colors. From a fleet of ships to an army of ants, her poetic presentation will challenge readers to consider other group-describing nouns as well.

New York: Grosset & Dunlap, 1987

Jewels

◖• A BEVY OF BOOKS •◗

Materials:

- •construction paper
- •pencils
- •crayons or markers

Lesson Procedure

1. Explain to students that they will be designing individual reading posters to record books that they read.
2. Suggest some collective nouns from *A Cache of Jewels* that might be appropriate.

   batch of books
   fleet of fiction
   muster of mysteries
   litter of literature
   string of stories
   host of humor (or history)
   bouquet of biographies

3. Invite each student to select a collective noun, create a reading slogan, and design an appropriate poster.
4. Display the reading posters on a bulletin board. As students read books, have them write the titles and authors on their posters.

Taking It Further . . .

Invite students to create bookmarks to match their reading posters. Students will enjoy exchanging bookmarks.

❧• MATCHING WORDS •❧

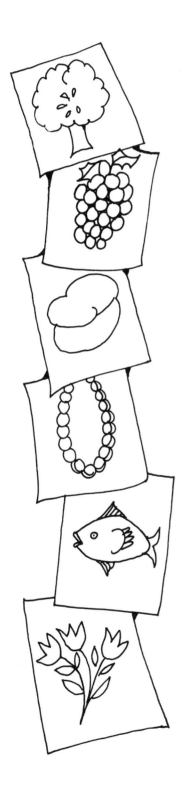

Materials:

- worksheets on pages 18-19
- 12" x 18" construction paper
- scissors
- glue

Lesson Procedure

1. Discuss any unfamiliar vocabulary in *A Cache of Jewels*.
2. Give each student a copy of both worksheets. Invite students to cut the word and picture cards apart.
3. Give each student a piece of construction paper. Have students glue each word card next to a matching picture card.

army/ants	cluster/grapes	pride/lions
batch/bread	fleet/ships	school/fish
bed/oysters	flock/sheep	string/pearls
bouquet/flowers	forest/trees	swarm/bees
bunch/bananas	litter/puppies	
clump/reeds	lock/hair	

Taking It Further . . .

Laminate a set of word and picture cards to make a memory game. Place all cards face down on a table. In turn, each student turns over two cards to match a picture with a word. If the cards match, the player keeps the pair and continues. If the cards do not match, they are turned back over and the next player tries to make a match.

army	batch	bed	bouquet
bunch	clump	cluster	fleet
flock	forest	litter	lock
pride	school	string	swarm

The Ruth Heller Connection © 1992 Fearon Teacher Aids

A Cache of Jewels

❧• NUMBER COLLECTIONS •❧

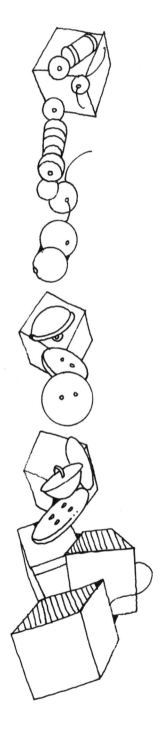

Materials:

•boxes of assorted counters (beads, blocks, buttons, beans)

Lesson Procedure

1. On the chalkboard, make a list of collective nouns used in math.

   pair
   set
   group
   sum
   product

2. Organize students into pairs or groups of 3 to 4 students. Give each group a box of counters.

3. Suggest story problems to the students and challenge them to select counters to illustrate the problems.

   A pair of blue marbles and a pair of green marbles makes a set of how many marbles?

   A group of three cars and a group of seven cars makes a group of how many cars?

Taking It Further . . .

Write number sentences on the chalkboard and invite students to create a story problem for each one.

A Cache of Jewels

Chickens

Ruth Heller challenges readers to think beyond birds when imagining creatures that lay eggs. She describes an interesting array of egg-laying reptiles, amphibians, fish, insects, and even mammals. The simple format is inviting to young readers and the intriguing content holds the attention of older readers.

New York: Grosset & Dunlap, 1981

Aren't the Only Ones

❦ • CREATIVE WRITING • ❦

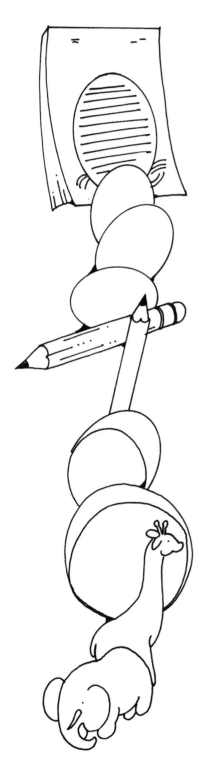

Materials:

- •worksheet on page 23
- •pencils
- •plastic eggs
- •miniature toy animals

Lesson Procedure

1. Before beginning the lesson, place one miniature animal (egg-laying bird, reptile, insect, or mammal) inside each plastic egg.
2. Have each student select an egg, but ask students not to open their eggs until the end of the activity.
3. Using the worksheet, invite each student to write a creative story about what might hatch from the egg. Students will be motivated by the intrigue of the unknown.
4. Encourage students to read their stories aloud for the class and then to "hatch" their eggs to discover what is really in them. Students will enjoy the surprise and comparing their predictions with the actual contents.

Taking It Further . . .

For a science activity, have each student open an egg and then write several clues about the enclosed animal on a 3" x 5" card. Clues might include zoological family, food, or habitat. Have students place the animals back inside the eggs and trade eggs and clue cards with another student. Invite students to read the clue cards and then guess what animal is in the egg they received.

Name _____

What's in the Egg?

• EGG ADDITION •

Materials:

- •lined paper
- •pencils
- •assorted colors, patterns, and sizes of plastic eggs
- •egg cartons

Lesson Procedure

1. Divide the class into groups of four. Give each group 10 to 20 assorted eggs and two or three egg cartons.
2. Invite students to categorize their eggs by color, size, or pattern and place them in the egg cartons accordingly.
3. Have students write sentences about their eggs.

> The number of red eggs is greater than
>   the number of green eggs.
> The number of plain eggs is equal to the
>   number of decorated eggs.

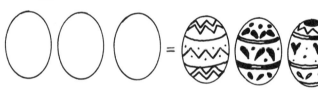

4. Encourage younger students to abbreviate the sentences or draw pictures instead of using words.

> red eggs > green eggs
> plain eggs = decorated eggs
> 2 red eggs + 3 blue eggs = 5 eggs

Taking It Further . . .

Give each student an egg carton. Encourage students to use eggs from their group collection to create addition number sentences. Students place 2 to 10 eggs in their cartons, draw a picture of each one, and write a number sentence describing the egg arrangement.

Chickens Aren't the Only Ones

EGG SIZE SORT

Materials:

•worksheet on page 26
•pencils
•reference books

Lesson Procedure

1. Discuss which bird lays the largest egg (ostrich) and which lays the smallest egg (hummingbird).
2. Encourage students to guess the size of both eggs. (An ostrich egg is about six inches in diameter and a hummingbird egg is about $1/2$ inch in diameter.)
3. Give each student a worksheet and invite students to guess the egg size of each bird. Have students write the names of the birds in order according to their egg size. Students should write the name of the bird that lays the smallest egg on the first line and the name of the bird that lays the largest egg on the last line.
4. After students have completed the worksheet, encourage them to use reference books to check their predictions and make adjustments to their answers.
5. Discuss some reasons why eggs vary in color, size, and shape. For example, some birds lay oval eggs because they are less likely to roll off a rocky ledge.

Answers to Worksheet

1. ruby-throated hummingbird (smallest)
2. bluebird
3. robin
4. starling
5. whippoorwill
6. crow
7. chicken
8. emperor penguin
9. emu
10. ostrich (largest)

Taking It Further . . .

Invite students to collect objects the approximate shape and size of the eggs laid by birds named on the worksheet. Organize the "eggs" into a museum exhibit in the classroom.

Name _____

Egg Size Sort

List the names of the birds in order by the size of egg each one lays (smallest to largest).

whippoorwill
ruby-throated hummingbird
robin
emu
starling

bluebird
ostrich
chicken
emperor penguin
crow

1. _____
       (smallest)

2. _____

3. _____

4. _____

5. _____

6. _____

7. _____

8. _____

9. _____

10. _____
       (largest)

The Ruth Heller Connection © 1992 Fearon Teacher Aids

EGG DROP

Materials:

•materials will vary

Lesson Procedure

1. Challenge students to design packaging for an egg so that it can be dropped without being broken.
2. Encourage students to be creative with materials and design ideas. The only rule students must follow is that the egg package cannot exceed 12" x 12" x 12".
3. Invite students to involve family members in the egg package design and production.
4. When all packages are complete, test the designs by dropping them from a designated height. (Out the window works well.)

Taking It Further . . .

After the test, invite students to work in groups of four to analyze the results revealed by the dropped packages. Have each group use the information to design a "new and improved" package. Students can test their new designs by dropping them from a greater height.

EGG ART

Materials:

- white egg
- bowl
- pin or needle
- egg dyes or food coloring
- egg-decorating materials (markers, crayons, yarn, and sequins)
- scissors
- glue

Lesson Procedure

1. Demonstrate how to blow out the inside of an egg. Send home the following instructions and ask students to return to school the next day with a blown egg from home.

   a. Using a pin or needle, make a pinhole through one end of an egg. Poke a larger hole ($^1/_8$") through the opposite end.
   b. Hold the egg so the larger hole is over a bowl. Blow hard through the smaller hole until the entire egg yolk and white falls into the bowl.
   c. Carefully run warm water into the larger hole and blow the water back out. Repeat until the inside of the shell is clean.
   d. Wrap the blown egg carefully in tissue paper.

2. Discuss some egg-decorating techniques, such as dying, etching, and applying appliques.
3. Provide a variety of egg-decorating materials or invite students to bring some supplies from home.
4. Invite students to decorate their blown eggs. Challenge students to cover the entire egg surface using three or more colors and two or more kinds of lines or shapes.

Taking It Further . . .

Students might enjoy reading *The Egg Tree* by Katherine Milhous (New York: Scribner's, 1950) and *Rechenka's Eggs* by Patricia Polacco (New York: Philomel, 1988).

Chickens Aren't the Only Ones

The Egyptian

Shirley Climo retells this ancient legend of a Greek slave girl who becomes queen after Pharaoh Amasis discovers that the rose-red slipper slides on her foot with ease. Ruth Heller brings the story to life with her brilliant illustrations.

Written by Shirley Climo
New York: Thomas Y. Crowell, 1989

Cinderella

THE MOST AMERICAN OF ALL

Materials:

• lined paper
• pencils

Lesson Procedure

1. Remind students of the Pharaoh's statement that Rhodopis was "the most Egyptian of all," even though the servant girls protested that she was not. Ask students to recall the reasons Pharaoh gave for this declaration.

   her eyes were as green as the Nile
   her hair as feathery as papyrus
   her skin the pink of a lotus flower

2. Discuss with students how America is a land of cultural diversity composed of immigrants from many lands. Ask students what they think makes someone an American. Challenge students to consider how each culture contributes to the richness of our common heritage. Encourage students to think beyond physical attributes of people as they consider the unique qualities of individuals.
3. Have each student write a list of his or her own unique qualities.
4. Invite students to write a paragraph in which they relate some of their qualities to familiar American symbols, just as Pharaoh related Rhodopis' appearance to Egyptian symbols. The paragraph may be entitled "Why I Am the Most American."

   At times, I drift through the day like the lazy Mississippi River.
   I often tumble into new adventures like the wreckless waters of Niagara Falls.

Taking It Further . . .

Give students a list of famous Americans from a variety of cultural backgrounds (Hank Aaron, Ralph Bunche, Cesar Chavez, Shirley Chisholm, Lee Trevino, Connie Chung, Jim Thorpe, Mary McLeod Bethune). Challenge individuals or cooperative learning groups of four to select one person from the list and research his or her background and achievements.

PYRAMID MATH

Materials:

- worksheet on page 32
- pencils

Lesson Procedure

1. Discuss the Egyptian setting of the story. Ask students to recall what they know about ancient Egypt. Point out that among many contributions in science, mathematics, and medicine, the ancient Egyptians built the pyramids, which are considered one of the "seven wonders of the world."
2. Give each pair of players a copy of the pyramid worksheet on page 32.
3. Explain to players that they will be building a math pyramid by writing and adding numbers in the bricks. Players take turns filling in a brick with a number from 1 to 15. (Each number can only be used once.)
4. After a player writes a number in a brick, he or she totals the score for that play by adding together the number just written with numbers in all adjacent bricks. (Adjacent bricks include all the bricks touching the brick in which the player just wrote a number.)

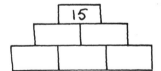

Player 1 would receive 15 points for this play.

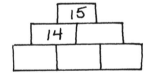

Player 2 would receive 29 points (14 + 15) for this play.

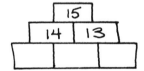

Player 1 would receive 42 points (13 + 14 + 15) for this play.

5. The player with the most points when all the bricks are filled is the winner.

Taking It Further . . .

To add an element of chance to the game, give each pair of players a pair of dice. Each player rolls the dice in turn and writes that number inside a brick.

Pyramid Math

Game 1

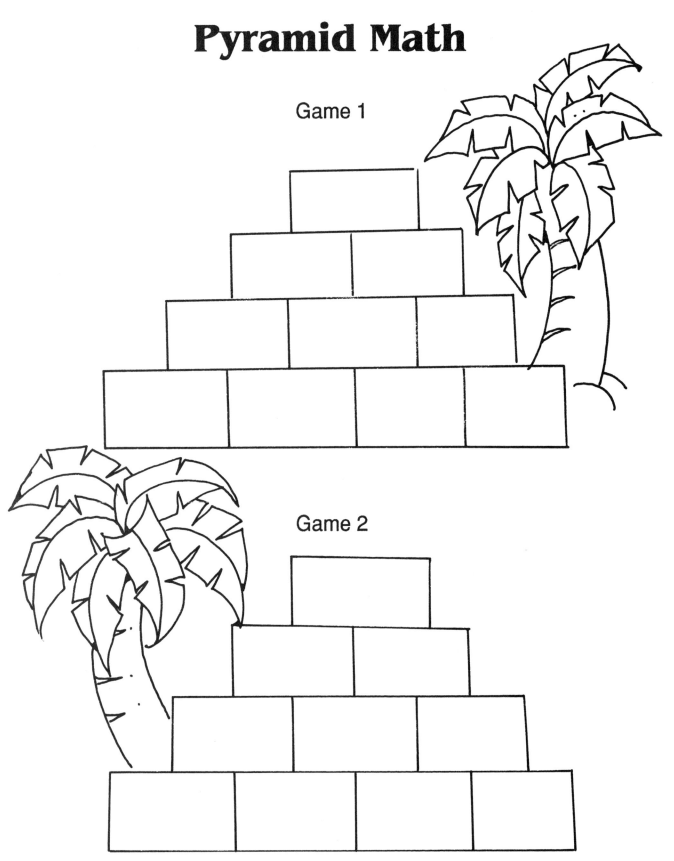

Game 2

The Egyptian Cinderella

The Ruth Heller Connection © 1992 Fearon Teacher Aids

 SCIENCE IN ANCIENT EGYPT

Materials:

• lined paper
• pencils
• encyclopedias and reference books

Lesson Procedure

1. Ask students to brainstorm what comes to mind when they think of ancient Egypt. Encourage students to recall the descriptions and illustrations from the story. Write responses on the chalkboard.
2. Explain to students that the early Egyptians contributed many discoveries in the areas of math and science. Their contributions influenced the cultures that followed.
3. Divide the class into cooperative learning groups of four students each. Challenge students to use research materials to find out what contributions the Egyptians made in one of the following areas.

calendar	bronze	embalming
geometry	surgery and medicine	paper
astronomy	glass	surveying

4. After the groups have had a few days to do their research, invite them to plan a presentation of their findings. Suggest that groups prepare a TV documentary, design a poster, or perform a skit.

Taking It Further . . .

Encourage students to find information about the important roles of some animals in ancient Egypt, such as those mentioned in the story—goose, monkey, hippopotamus, and falcon.

• COLOR A COLLAR •

Materials:

- •18" x 18" white construction paper
- •pencils
- •colored pencils, markers, crayons, or paint

Lesson Procedure

1. Point out some of the ornate collars worn by the Egyptians as illustrated in the story. These collars were made of gold, jewels, or beads and worn as decoration by those who could afford them.
2. Give each student an 18" x 18" sheet of white paper.
3. Have each student fold the sheet of paper in half diagonally three times to make a triangle.
4. Have students measure four inches from the folded point and draw a curved line from one side to the other. Have students cut on this line.
5. Have students measure about four inches from the cut line and mark. Cut another curved line from side to side.
6. When students unfold the paper, it should look like a doughnut (some may have slightly scalloped edges).
7. Students can design patterns on their collars with pencil. Encourage the use of repetition and simple geometric shapes and lines.
8. Invite students to color the completed designs. Cut a slit in each collar so students can wear them.

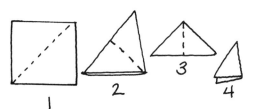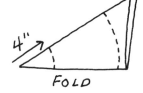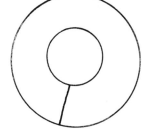

Taking It Further . . .

Invite students to wear their Egyptian collars for a parade throughout the school. Or, use the collars as picture frames for stories or book reports.

The Egyptian Cinderella

☙• EGYPTIAN ART TECHNIQUES •☙

Materials:

• drawing paper
• pencils
• colored pencils, markers, or crayons

Lesson Procedure

1. Discuss some of the characteristics of ancient Egyptian art.

   Paintings showed scenes from life on earth as well as activities enjoyed by the deceased, such as hunting and fishing.

   Paintings often included rows or columns of hieroglyphics describing the achievements of the subject.

   Strict rules were followed for the portrayal of human figures. The head, hips, and legs were shown in profile. The eye and torso were shown with a frontal view. Men were usually painted brown and women were painted yellow.

   Plants and animals were often portrayed in paintings.

   Important subjects were drawn larger than other objects in the picture.

2. Challenge students to find examples in the book where Ruth Heller adheres to these rules. For example, she has included many plants and animals and the Pharaoh is portrayed larger than other figures.

3. Encourage students to draw pictures of themselves Egyptian-style using the following criteria.

   Make yourself the focus by drawing your image the largest.

   Include scenes of you involved in some of your favorite activities.

   Include symbols representing accomplishments in your life.

   Remember the rules for portraying the human figure.

Taking It Further . . .

Discuss the Egyptian belief that the deceased could take things with them into the afterlife. Explain the practice the wealthy had of filling tombs with material possessions. Encourage students to list 3 to 5 possessions they would want to always keep by their side.

The Egyptian Cinderella

☙ • CINDERELLA STORIES • ☙

Materials:

• various versions of the Cinderella story

Lesson Procedure

1. On the chalkboard, list some of the elements of a Cinderella story.

   Cinderella is poor and mistreated.
   There is a step-family.
   There is a fairy godmother or other magical character.
   A shoe is an important part of the story.
   A royal person falls in love with Cinderella.

2. Read and compare different versions of Cinderella. Read the stories aloud to the class or assign cooperative learning groups to read and analyze different versions and report their findings to the class.

   Clark, Ann Nolan. *In the Land of Small Dragon:*
     A Vietnamese Folktale. New York: Viking, 1979.
   Hooks, William H. *Moss Gown.* New York: Clarion, 1987.
   Louie, Ai-Ling. *Yeh-Shen: A Cinderella Story from China.*
     New York: Philomel, 1982.
   Steel, Flora Annie. *Tattercoats.* New York: Bradbury Press,
     1976.

Taking It Further . . .

Challenge students to rewrite another well-known fairytale, such as *Little Red Riding Hood, The Three Bears,* or *The Three Billy Goats Gruff,* in an ancient Egyptian setting.

The Egyptian Cinderella

· SHOES ·

Materials:

- •worksheet on page 38
- •pencils
- •shoes

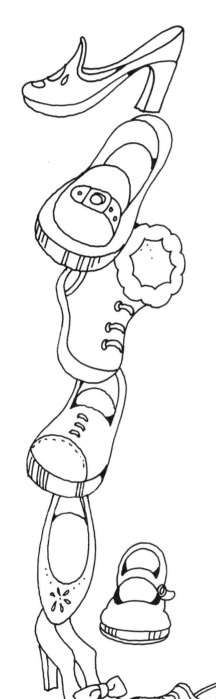

Lesson Procedure

1. Ask each student to bring a favorite shoe to school.
2. Discuss the significance of the slipper in the Cinderella story.
3. Give each student a worksheet and ask students to write about their favorite shoe. Students can include a description of the shoe, how the shoe was acquired, and why the shoe is so special.
4. Arrange the completed shoe worksheets on a bulletin board.
5. Display the shoes on a table next to the bulletin board. Challenge students to match each shoe with its description.

Taking It Further . . .

Play a game of "Cinderella Shoe." Hold up one shoe at a time. Challenge three students (one being the real owner) to claim the shoe and tell why it is their favorite. Invite the class to guess who is the real owner.

The Egyptian Cinderella

My Favorite Shoe

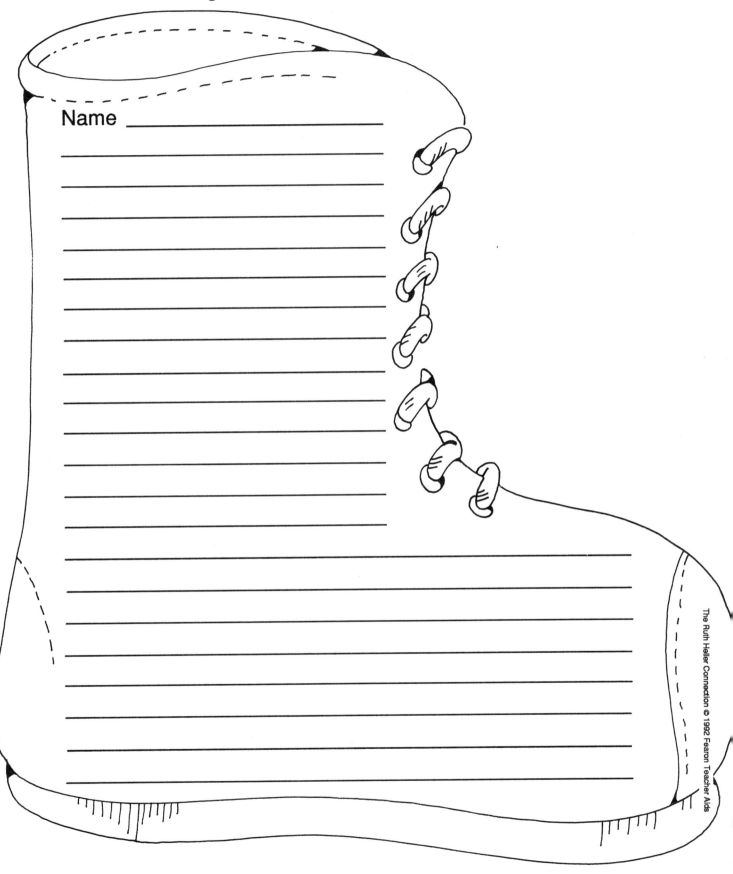

Name _____

The Egyptian Cinderella

How to Hide

Just one in a series of easy-to-hold 6" x 6" books, this tale takes readers on a fascinating hide-and-seek journey through the world of camouflage.

New York: Grosset & Dunlap, 1985

a Butterfly & Other Insects

✏ • DON'T HIDE THE FACTS! • ✏

Materials:

• worksheet on page 41
• other Ruth Heller books:

> *How to Hide a Crocodile & Other Reptiles,* 1986
> *How to Hide a Gray Treefrog & Other Amphibians,* 1986
> *How to Hide a Whippoorwill & Other Birds,* 1986
> *How to Hide an Octopus & Other Sea Creatures,* 1986

• pencils
• reference books

Lesson Procedure

1. Read Ruth Heller's other books in the camouflage series or display them at a center for students to read independently.
2. Invite students to select a creature from one of the books and do research to find out some hidden facts about it.
3. Students can use the worksheet lines to record the facts they have uncovered and draw a picture of their creature in the box.
4. Encourage students to read their completed reports aloud to the class. Challenge classmates to guess what creature the facts describe.

Taking It Further . . .

Invite students to write one fact about their creature on a lift-up flap covering a picture of the creature. Display the facts on a bulletin board. Encourage students to read the clue, guess the creature, and then lift the flap to see if their guess is accurate.

How to Hide a Butterfly & Other Insects

Don't Hide the Facts!

Choose a camouflage creature from one of Ruth Heller's books. Use reference books to discover some hidden facts about it. Write the facts on the lines provided. Draw a picture of your creature inside the box.

My Creature _____

Hidden Facts

_____

_____

_____

_____

_____

_____

PATTERNS FROM NATURE

Materials:

- *Designs for Coloring: Butterflies* by Ruth Heller, 1985
- nature prints
- drawing paper
- crayons or markers

Lesson Procedure

1. Discuss how patterns in nature help to create protective camouflage. Invite students to look at nature prints and point out special designs. Suggest that students look particularly closely at patterns in insects, flowers, and plants.
2. Show students some of the designs and patterns in the book *Designs for Coloring: Butterflies* and invite students to draw a butterfly or other insect. Encourage students to concentrate on a pattern when decorating it. Suggest that students get ideas from patterns in nature.

Taking it Further . . .

Divide the class into groups of four. Give each group an environmental print showing a natural setting, such as a desert, forest, meadow, or shoreline. Ask students to design insects that might live in the environment shown.

How to Hide a Butterfly & Other Insects

How to Hide a

Another in the miniature series of camouflage readers, this book invites children to explore the mysteries of hidden mammals.

New York: Grosset & Dunlap, 1985

Polar Bear & Other Mammals

☙ • CAMOUFLAGE WRITING • ☙

Materials:

•worksheet on page 46
•lined paper
•pencils

Lesson Procedure

1. Discuss how different animals use camouflage to hide. Ask the students to share some examples.
2. Tell the students that they are going to do camouflage writing. Camouflage writing is descriptive writing in which the writer tells about a person, place, or object without revealing its identity. Mystery writers use this technique to develop characters, settings, and plots.
3. Give each student a copy of the worksheet on page 46. Invite students to select a topic. Suggest that students think of someone or something in the room, a person or place in their social studies books, or a book character.
4. Instruct students to make a list of attributes of their subject.
5. Encourage students to use their lists to write descriptive paragraphs about their subjects. Remind writers to begin with the most subtle descriptions and save the most obvious attributes for the end of the story.

Standing alone against a far wall, little and gray, I might appear unimportant and unimpressive to all of you. You laugh at my bloated stomach and my strange appetite for wood. Still, I notice that you cannot resist my one crooked arm. None of you can keep from touching it and twirling it. Chuckle as you may about my unusual diet, all of you like to feed me. I have noticed that some of you have sampled my food yourselves! For some of you, your fascination goes beyond my eating habits. Besides testing how quickly I can grind up my food, you often feel the need to examine the contents of my stomach before emptying it. Yes, you ignore me hanging over here out of the way until your curiosity gets the best of you. Or until you need a sharper pencil.

6. Ask students to share their camouflage writing with the class. Challenge classmates to identify the subject of each paragraph.

Taking It Further . . .

Encourage students to write about a time when they tried to "blend in" with their surroundings in order to avoid being noticed. Or, challenge students to think of creative ways to stand out and be unique.

Camouflage Writing

1. Choose a person, place, or object.

   _____

2. On the back of this paper, list attributes of your subject.
3. Use your list to write a paragraph describing your subject without naming it. Remember to begin with the most subtle descriptions and save the most obvious attributes for the end.

_____

_____

_____

_____

_____

_____

_____

_____

_____

_____

_____

_____

_____

How to Hide a Polar Bear & Other Mammals

The Ruth Heller Connection © 1992 Fearon Teacher Aids

King of the

When chaos reigns among the birds, owl devises a contest to fairly decide who will be king. Enhanced by Ruth Heller's magnificent paintings, Shirley Climo retells one of the world's oldest legends with humor and wit.

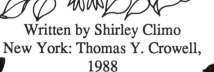

Written by Shirley Climo
New York: Thomas Y. Crowell,
1988

Birds

❧• PERSUASIVE WRITING •❧

Materials:

•lined paper
•pencils

Lesson Procedure

1. Ask students to recall each bird's reason for wanting to become king.

   Skylark: "Everyone listens to my sweet voice."
   Peacock: "I am the one with something worth showing off."
   Raven: "Since I am so clever, I should be king."
   Falcon: "Respect is what's necessary."

2. Discuss the birds' ideas of what makes a good leader and ask students if they agree or disagree.
3. Invite students to brainstorm their own list of good leadership qualities. Write the list on the chalkboard.
4. Invite students to choose one leadership quality from the list that they possess. Encourage students to write a persuasive speech explaining why they should be a class leader based on their possession of that quality.

Taking It Further . . .

Hold elections for class offices and encourage students to participate in a persuasive campaign based on their knowledge of good leadership. Encourage voters to consider each candidates' leadership qualities when voting.

King of the Birds

CREATIVE WRITING

Materials:

- worksheet on page 50
- pencils
- reference books

Lesson Procedure

1. Challenge students to create new titles for a retelling of the story, *King of the Birds*, using a different setting and animal family.

   Monarch of the Mammals
   Queen of the Sea
   Regent of the Reptiles
   Boss of the Bugs

2. Invite students to select a topic and then list some animals they might include in their stories. For example, a "Monarch of the Mammals" story might include:

   A giraffe who thinks the ruler should be able to see over everyone else.
   A rhinoceros who boasts that he has a tough armor.
   A mouse who points out that his small size is advantageous for spying.

3. Encourage students to use their lists to create a new version of *King of the Birds*.

Taking It Further . . .

Point out the inferences made in the story explaining why certain birds look or act as they do today—for example, Stork rested on one leg, Ostrich refused to fly again, and Wren's tail points toward the sky. Challenge students to explain the peculiar looks or behavior of other animals through a fictional story. Students will also enjoy hearing some of Kipling's *Just So Stories*.

Another King

_____
_____
_____
_____
_____
_____
_____
_____
_____
_____
_____
_____
_____
_____
_____
_____
_____
_____

The Ruth Heller Connection © 1992 Fearon Teacher Aids

Kites

Kites sail high and so will imaginations in this vivid verb adventure. Readers will explore the sounds and meanings of verbs as well as their many uses. From helping verbs to the subjunctive mood, readers will march, climb, leap, and slither through the pages.

New York: Grosset & Dunlap, 1988

Sail High

• VERBS •

Materials:

- worksheet on page 53
- pencils
- thesaurus

Lesson Procedure

1. Ask students to recall some of the nouns that Ruth Heller uses to link with verbs.

   Roses bloom.
   People run.
   Pelicans fly.
   Kites sail.
   Rabbits multiply.

2. Encourage students to think of additional verbs that make sense with each noun.

   Roses grow.
   Roses climb.
   Roses wilt.
   Roses nod.

3. On the worksheet, encourage students to write mini-sentences by listing new verbs for each noun. Challenge students to write as many verbs as possible. Students can use a thesaurus for additional ideas.

Taking It Further . . .

Invite students to design verb posters. In the middle of a large sheet of drawing paper, students draw an illustration of a noun. In their best handwriting or calligraphy, have students write matching verbs around the illustration.

Verbs

Write as many mini-sentences as you can for each noun. How many different verbs can you use?

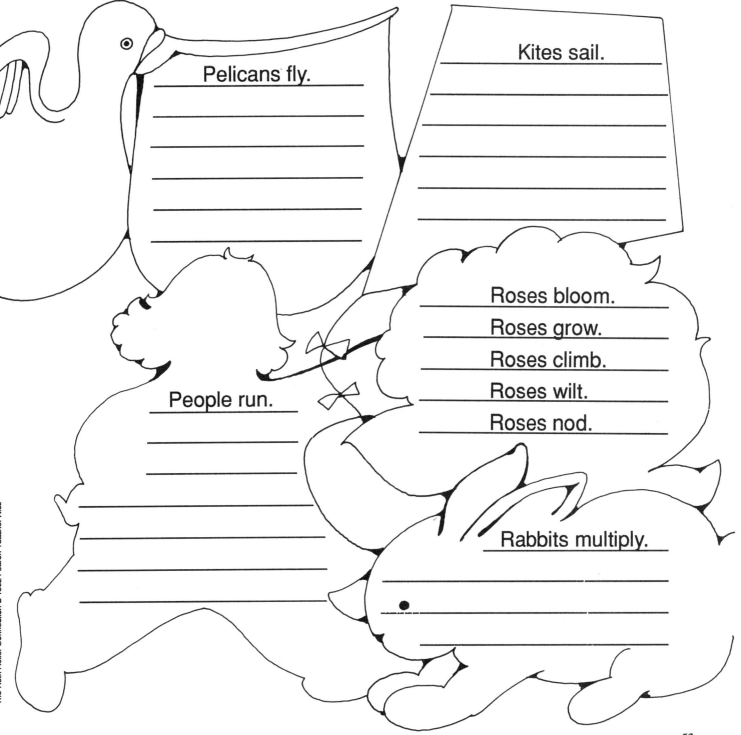

Pelicans fly.

Kites sail.

Roses bloom.
Roses grow.
Roses climb.
Roses wilt.
Roses nod.

People run.

Rabbits multiply.

Kites Sail High

• VERB TENSES •

Materials:

•worksheet on page 55
•pencils

sing sang sung grow grew grown fly flew flown give gave given

Lesson Procedure

1. Explain to students that verb tenses deal with time— past, present, and future. Discuss how we use the past tense to talk about what happened yesterday, the present tense to talk about today, and the future tense to talk about what will happen tomorrow.
2. Using the worksheet, have students fill in each blank in the middle column (Today) with a verb. Students can gather verbs from the story, independent reading, or a student-generated list on the chalkboard.
3. Invite students to fill in the left-hand column with the past tense form of each verb and the right-hand column with the future tense form of each verb.

Taking It Further . . .

This activity can be especially beneficial to ESL students. Keep extra copies of the worksheet available. Then ask students to record verbs they come across in reading or writing assignments. Assist students in filling in the past and future tenses of each verb.

Verb Tenses

Yesterday (past tense)	Today (present tense)	Tomorrow (future tense)
bloomed	*bloom*	*will bloom*

The Ruth Heller Connection © 1992 Fearon Teacher Aids

☙ • VIGOROUS VERBS • ❧

Materials:

Lesson Procedure

1. Ask students to recall the "vigorous verbs" used in the story.

   Fireworks EXPLODE.
   Horses THUNDER down the road.

2. Ask students to name some familiar verbs that they commonly use. Make a list of these verbs on the chalkboard under the title "Easy Actions."

3. Challenge students to think of some vigorous verbs that express each easy action more dramatically.

Easy Actions	Vigorous Verbs
run	thunder, dash, scamper
walk	amble, trudge, stomp
talk	chatter, shout, drawl
fly	sail, skim, soar
play	romp, frolic, fiddle

4. Remind students how helpful a thesaurus can be when looking for another way to say something. Encourage students to use a thesaurus in their daily writing.

Taking It Further . . .

Ask students to circle easy action verbs in a sample of their own writing. Challenge them to replace each circled word with a vigorous verb.

56

IN THE MOOD

Materials:

- worksheet on page 58
- pencils

Lesson Procedure

1. Remind students of the three moods verbs can express as mentioned in the story and give an example of each.

   The *imperative mood* makes a request or gives a command.
   Please come here.
   Sit down!

   The *indicative mood* states a fact.
   We read.

   The *subjunctive mood* expresses a wish. It often uses the words "as though" or "if."
   If I were a bird, I would fly all day.

2. Using the worksheet, ask students to write three sentences for each picture using each of the three verb moods. For the first picture, students might write:

   JUMP in the net, fish. (Imperative)
   That fish SWIMS fast. (Indicative)
   If my fish HAD a bigger bowl, he WOULD BE happier. (Subjunctive)

Taking It Further . . .

Challenge students to find examples of different verb moods as they read and share them with the class. Or, as you read together in groups or as a class, point out verbs and ask students to identify the mood.

Name _____

In the Mood

Write three sentences for each picture. Write one sentence in the *imperative mood*, one in the *indicative mood,* and one in the *subjunctive mood*.

The *imperative mood* makes a request or gives a command.
   Please come here.
   Sit down!
The *indicative mood* states a fact.
   We read.
The *subjunctive mood* expresses a wish. It often uses the words "as though" or "if."
   If I were a bird, I would fly all day.

_____
_____
_____

_____
_____
_____

_____
_____
_____

The Ruth Heller Connection © 1992 Fearon Teacher Aids

Kites Sail High

VOICES OF VERBS

Materials

- worksheet on page 60
- pencils

Lesson Procedure

1. Remind students that verbs have two voices—active and passive. Write the examples from the story of active and passive voices on the chalkboard.

   This egg was laid by a hen named Sade.
   A hen named Sade laid this egg.

2. Ask students to analyze both sentences. Explain to students that in the passive voice, the subject is acted upon, as in the first example. The subject (egg) was acted upon (was laid). In the active voice, the subject is doing the action, as in the second example. The subject (Sade) did the action (laid this egg).

3. Write the following sentences on the chalkboard. Ask students to identify whether the verb voice is active or passive. If the voice is passive, then change it to active, and if the voice is active, then change it to passive.

   The dog caught the thief. (Active)
   Change to: The thief was caught by the dog. (Passive)
   She grilled the hamburger over the flame. (Active)
   Change to: The hamburger was grilled over the flame. (Passive)
   The mail was delivered by Sam. (Passive)
   Change to: Sam delivered the mail. (Active)

4. On the worksheet, challenge students to write two sentences for each picture using active and passive verb voices.

Taking It Further . . .

Encourage students to identify examples of verb voices as they read.

Name _____

Voices of Verbs

Write two sentences for each picture. Use the *active voice*
for one sentence and the *passive voice* for the other.

_____

_____

_____

_____

_____

_____

_____

_____

The Ruth Heller Connection © 1992 Fearon Teacher Aids

Kites Sail High

❮❭ VERB PICTURES ❮❭

Materials:

- drawing paper
- pencils
- crayons or markers

Lesson Procedure

1. On the chalkboard, list several of the verbs that Ruth Heller uses in *Kites Sail High*.

leap	cavort	thunder
slither	multiply	paint
splash	explode	march
creep		

2. Instruct students to fold a sheet of drawing paper in half three times. The paper will have eight boxes when opened.
3. Ask students to write a verb from the chalkboard or one of their own in each box.
4. Invite students to illustrate each verb with a simple picture.

Taking It Further . . .

Give each student eight 3" x 5" cards. Encourage students to write a verb on four of the cards and to draw corresponding pictures on the other four cards. Collect the cards, mix them up, and challenge the class to match verbs with their illustrations.

❧• PERSONAL VERBS •❧

Materials:

- lined paper
- pencils

Lesson Procedure

1. Time students for three minutes as they quickly write down a list of as many verbs as they can think of.
2. Encourage students to read some of the verbs from their lists to the class.
3. Repeat the activity allowing students an additional three minutes to add more verbs to their lists.
4. Ask students to circle the verbs on their lists that describe something they do personally. Give students an opportunity to share their "personal verbs."

Taking It Further . . .

Give each student an 18" x 24" sheet of construction paper. Invite students to make posters illustrating their personal verbs.

Many Luscious

"An adjective's terrific when you want to be specific." With imaginative poetry and brilliantly true-to-life pictures, Ruth Heller explores the world of adjectives. This beautiful and informative picture book shows children how much fun words can be.

New York: Grosset & Dunlap, 1989

Lollipops

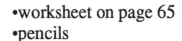

❧ • ADJECTIVE SQUARES • ❧

Materials:

• worksheet on page 65
• pencils

Lesson Procedure

1. Ask students to recall, from the book, what type of words adjectives can describe.

person	thing
place	thoughts, ideas, or emotions

2. Invite students to write the name of a person, place, thing, or thought in each square on the worksheet.

skater	shoe	happiness
carnival	opinion	

3. Have students trade papers. Encourage students to fill in each box on their partners' papers with an adjective that describes the noun.

graceful skater	thoughtful opinion
glittery carnival	extreme happiness
raggedy shoe	

Taking It Further . . .

Invite students to trade papers again. Have the students write sentences for each pair of words on the back of the worksheets. Then return papers to their original owners.

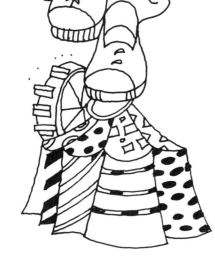

64

Adjective Squares

☙• WEATHER WATCH •☙

Materials:

- •calendar
- •markers

Lesson Procedure

1. Each morning, ask students to brainstorm a list of adjectives that describe the weather. List the suggestions on the chalkboard.

wet	cloudy	exciting
soggy	gray	crisp
drizzly	bright	wintery
rainy	cheerful	peaceful

2. Invite a student-of-the-day to choose one adjective to describe the morning and write it on the calendar.
3. Repeat this same process each day for one month.
4. At the end of the month, invite students to use some of the adjectives on the calendar to write a weather poem. Encourage students to use original adjectives as well.

Taking It Further . . .

Invite each student to select one day from the calendar and illustrate the weather-watch word on a 3" x 3" square of tagboard. Attach the squares to an 18" x 24" sheet of colored construction paper to make a picture calendar of the month.

Many Luscious Lollipops

SUPERLATIVE MATH

Materials:

•worksheet on page 68
•yard sticks, meter sticks, or rulers
•pencils

Lesson Procedure

1. Ask students to recall the *comparatives* and *superlatives* Ruth Heller used in *Many Luscious Lollipops*.

   curly, curlier, curliest
   fair, fairer, fairest

2. Remind students that -er is added for a comparative and -est is added for a superlative.
3. Make a list of some comparatives and superlatives that are used in math.

   long, longer, longest
   wide, wider, widest
   tall, taller, tallest
   thick, thicker, thickest
   far, farther, farthest
   big, bigger, biggest

4. Invite students to fill in the blanks on the worksheet to make comparisons between objects in the classroom. Have students use their measuring skills to record the length, width, height, thickness, or distance of each object to verify their comparisons. The students' answers will vary.

   The <u>table</u> is long. It is <u>6 feet.</u>
   The <u>chalkboard</u> is longer. It is <u>12 feet.</u>
   The <u>bulletin board</u> is longest. It is <u>25 feet.</u>

Taking It Further . . .

Challenge students to search their math books for more examples of comparatives and superlatives, such as "Seven is <u>greater</u> than three" or "Which area is the <u>smallest</u>?"

Name _____

Superlative Math

Fill in the blank of the first sentence with the name of
an object or a person in the classroom. Write the
measurement for each object or person in the second
blank.

The <u>table</u> is *long*. It is <u>6 feet</u>.
The <u>chalkboard</u> is *longer*. It is <u>12 feet</u>.
The <u>bulletin board</u> is *longest*. It is <u>25 feet</u>.

The _____ is *wide*. It is _____ .
The _____ is *wider*. It is _____ .
The _____ is *widest*. It is _____ .

_____ is *tall*. He/she is _____ .
_____ is *taller*. He/she is _____ .
_____ is *tallest*. He/she is _____ .

The _____ is *thick*. It is _____ .
The _____ is *thicker*. It is _____ .
The _____ is *thickest*. It is _____ .

_____ sits *far* from me. His/her desk is
_____ away.
_____ sits *farther* from me. His/her desk is
_____ away.
_____ sits *farthest* from me. His/her desk is
_____ away.

The Ruth Heller Connection © 1992 Fearon Teacher Aids

ADJECTIVE SELF PORTRAIT

Materials:

- worksheet on page 70
- pencils
- construction paper

Lesson Procedure

1. After giving each student a worksheet, discuss the types of adjectives that would be appropriate for each blank.

   hair—curly, straight, silky, shiny, brown
   personality—kind, outgoing, quiet, helpful
   mood—happy, thoughtful, calm, rebellious, wild
   movement—slow, graceful, thunderous, snappy
   conversation—humorous, wise, soft, precise
   talent—artistic, athletic, clever, musical
   some people think—energetic, funny, independent

2. Invite students to complete the self-portrait worksheet to describe themselves.
3. Encourage students to draw the outline of their hair around the head.
4. Mount the self portraits on brightly-colored construction paper and display them on a bulletin board.

Taking It Further . . .

Read some of the self portraits aloud and invite the class to guess who the adjectives describe. Or, encourage students to write an adjective portrait about a friend. Emphasize that the portraits be positive and complimentary.

My hair is _____ .

I am a _____ person.

I am usually in a _____ mood.

My movement is _____ .

My conversation is usually _____ .

I am _____ .

Some people think I am _____ .

Name _____

❧ • SUPERLATIVE COLORS • ❧

Materials:

- •worksheet on page 72
- •pencils
- •magazines
- •scissors
- •glue

Lesson Procedure

1. Discuss various attributes of color. Show students some magazine pictures, book illustrations, or paintings that illustrate these attributes.

   value—lightness and darkness (lightness or tint is created by adding white, darkness or shade is created by adding black)
   cool colors—greens, blues, violets
   warm colors—yellows, oranges, reds
   neutral colors—brown, black, gray, white
   intensity—how bright or pure the color is

2. Invite students to select one attribute and write it along with its comparative and superlative forms on the lines below each box on the worksheet.

   cool, cooler, coolest
   bright, brighter, brightest
   dark, darker, darkest
   white, whiter, whitest

3. Ask students to look in magazines for examples of the attribute they chose. Have students cut out and glue one picture in each box to accurately portray the comparison they have chosen.

Taking It Further . . .

Label a large piece of butcher paper with different color attributes. Encourage students to keep alert for examples to attach to the mural. This will turn your students into art detectives.

Name _____

Superlative Colors

The Ruth Heller Connection © 1992 Fearon Teacher Aids

Many Luscious Lollipops

Merry-Go-Round

This striking addition to Ruth Heller's series on language transforms nouns from the mundane to the marvelous. The winsome words and stunning illustrations create a new look at people, places, and things.

New York: Grosset & Dunlap, 1990

THE NOUN GAME

Materials:

- lined paper
- pencils

Lesson Procedure

1. Explain to students that the object of the game is to create new nouns by adding, subtracting, or changing a letter, blend, or consonant combination in an existing word.
2. Divide the class into pairs. Give each pair of players a sheet of lined paper and ask them to number the sheet from 1 to 20 down the left-hand side.
3. The first player begins the game by writing a one-syllable noun on the first numbered line of the paper.
4. The second player makes a new noun by adding, subtracting, or changing a letter, blend, or consonant combination and writes the new noun on the second numbered line. The player receives two points for this play.

   cat
   cart (add r)

5. Players continue to create new words in turn.

   cat
   cart
   card (change t to d)
   lard (change c to l)

6. The game ends when players reach the last line, in which case, a tie is declared. If a player is unable to make a new noun before reaching the last line, the player who wrote the last noun wins.

Taking It Further . . .

Discuss how home economists often write columns sharing ways to use common objects in the home. Invite students to choose a common object in the classroom or a noun from the "Noun Game" and list several ways it could be used in the classroom. For example, a door handle could be used to store rubberbands, mold clay pots, or hang coats.

❦ • PLURAL NOUNS • ❦

Materials:

•worksheet on page 76
•pencils

Lesson Procedure

1. Remind students how most plural nouns are made by adding -s or -es.
2. Challenge students to create as many nouns as possible by connecting letters on the worksheet horizontally, vertically, or diagonally. Each letter can be used only once in a word. Point out that there are many s's and es's to add to words to make them longer.
3. Players can keep track of their score as words are found. Players receive one point for a 3- or 4-letter word, two points for a 5-letter word, three points for a 6-letter word, and four points for a 7-letter word.

Taking It Further . . .

Students can make their own game cards on one-inch grid paper. Outline or cut a 4" x 5" card. Fill in three e's and five s's randomly. Fill the remaining twelve squares with random vowels and consonants.

Noun Find

Create as many nouns as possible by connecting letters horizontally, vertically, or diagonally. Each letter can be used only once in a word.

C	A	N	A	C
A	R	S	F	E
T	E	E	I	S
S	O	H	S	P

Noun Find

Create as many nouns as possible by connecting letters horizontally, vertically, or diagonally. Each letter can be used only once in a word.

C	A	N	A	C
A	R	S	F	E
T	E	E	I	S
S	O	H	S	P

❧ PAPER-PLATE MERRY-GO-ROUND ☙

Materials:

- •worksheet on page 78
- •4" x 24" strips of construction paper
- •paper plates
- •crayons or markers
- •rulers
- •pencils
- •clear tape

Lesson Procedure

1. Give each child a 4" x 24" strip of construction paper. Help students measure and mark the strips to indicate the merry-go-round posts using the following dimensions. For primary students, measuring may need to be done in advance.

2"	4"	4"	4"	4"	4"	2"

2. Invite students to draw six horses on their paper strips following the step-by-step instructions provided on the worksheet. You might want to demonstrate on the chalkboard how the finished product will look. Be sure students center each horse over a post. Encourage students to add decorative detail to make each horse unique.

3. Tape the ends of the paper strips together to create a circle.
4. Give each student two paper plates. Have students color the bottom of one plate.
5. Assemble the merry-go-round by taping the colored plate to the top of the circular paper strip and the plain plate to the bottom of the paper strip.

Taking It Further . . .

Invite students to choose one of their merry-go-round horses and write about a magical ride they take on it.

Merry-Go-Round Horse

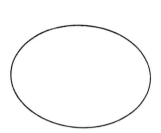

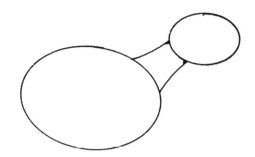

1. Make a watermelon shape for a body.

2. Make a smaller watermelon shape for a head. Connect the two ovals with a neck.

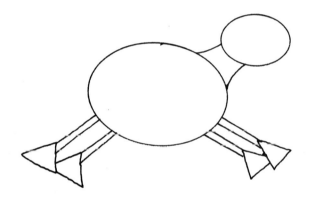

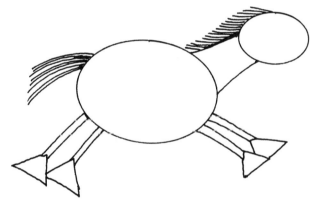

3. Add four legs with triangles on the ends for hooves.

4. Add lines for the tail and mane.

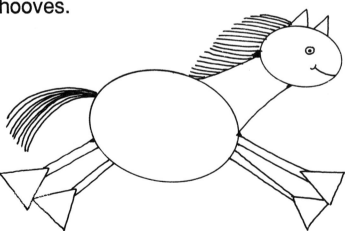

5. Add ears, an eye, and a mouth.

The Ruth Heller Connection © 1992 Fearon Teacher Aids

Merry-Go-Round

Plants That

Scientifically accurate and visually compelling, this beautiful book is packed with interesting facts about mushrooms, seaweed, moss, and other plants that never ever bloom.

New York: Grosset & Dunlap, 1984

Never Ever Bloom

❧• PINECONE DERBY •❧

Materials:

- worksheet on page 81
- pinecones
- assorted sticks, paper clips, and washers
- assorted paper and cardboard
- scissors
- glue
- masking tape
- wire

Lesson Procedure

1. Explain to students that they will each be designing a race car from a pinecone. The cars will be raced to see which car can be pushed the farthest.
2. Invite students to explore the available materials and create a pinecone race car.
3. When the cars are completed, ask each student to fill out the entry form on the worksheet.
4. Use masking tape to mark a starting line on the floor. Invite each race entrant to push his or her car past the starting line with one big push. Students' hands cannot cross the starting line.
5. Mark the spot where each car stops. The car that travels the farthest is the winner of the derby.

Taking It Further . . .

Invite students to write newspaper articles reporting on the Pinecone Derby.

Pinecone Derby

· ENTRY FORM ·

Race Car Name _____

Race Car Number _____

Car's Owner _____

City _____ State _____

Date _____

Sponsor _____
(signature of parent, teacher, or principal)

Driver _____

_____
(Derby Official)

Plants That Never Ever Bloom

GYMNOPRINTS

Materials:

- drawing paper
- tempera paint in paper cups or plastic containers
- paintbrushes
- newspaper
- gymnosperms (sliced mushrooms, moss, ferns, needles from conifers, ginkgo leaves)

Lesson Procedure

1. Remind students that plants that never ever bloom are classified as *gymnosperms*. Show the gymnosperm examples you have collected.
2. Explain to students that they will be making art prints using gymnosperms and paint.
3. Cover desks with newspaper and hand out drawing paper, paint, and brushes.
4. Invite students to select several gymnosperms for printmaking.
5. Encourage students to arrange the plants on their drawing paper to create an interesting design.
6. Have students lift one plant at a time and lightly paint one side of it with tempera paint.
7. Have students carefully replace the plants, painted side down, on the drawing paper. Students cover the plants with another sheet of drawing paper and press firmly.
8. Invite students to carefully lift each plant off the drawing paper, being careful not to smear the prints. When all the plants are removed, a painted gymnoprint will remain. Allow the prints to dry thoroughly.

Taking It Further . . .

Challenge students to propose a theory about why most gymnosperms live in dark places and most flower-bearing plants live where there is more light.

☙• MUSHROOM MADNESS •❧

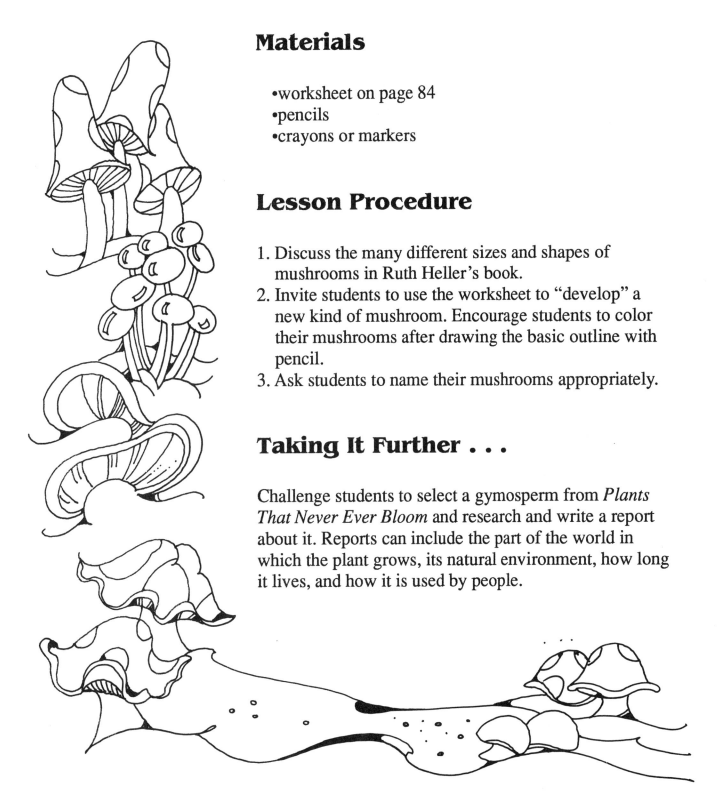

Materials

- worksheet on page 84
- pencils
- crayons or markers

Lesson Procedure

1. Discuss the many different sizes and shapes of mushrooms in Ruth Heller's book.
2. Invite students to use the worksheet to "develop" a new kind of mushroom. Encourage students to color their mushrooms after drawing the basic outline with pencil.
3. Ask students to name their mushrooms appropriately.

Taking It Further . . .

Challenge students to select a gymosperm from *Plants That Never Ever Bloom* and research and write a report about it. Reports can include the part of the world in which the plant grows, its natural environment, how long it lives, and how it is used by people.

Mushroom Madness

Scientist, _____ ,
has recently discovered a new mushroom named
_____ .

The Ruth Heller Connection © 1992 Fearon Teacher Aids

Plants That Never Ever Bloom

The Reason for

From the tiniest speck of pollen to the huge Rafflesia, Ruth Heller explores why flowers are necessary. With poetic style and bold illustrations, this stunning science book beautifully portrays the importance of flower-bearing plants.

New York: Grosset & Dunlap, 1983

a Flower

❧• I ATE THE WHOLE THING •❧

Materials:

•lined paper
•pencils

Lesson Procedure

1. Give students an opportunity to look again at the illustrations in Ruth Heller's book to notice the many plant parts that we eat, such as seeds (corn) and roots (radishes).
2. Make six columns on the chalkboard and list one of the following plant parts at the top of each column.

Flower	Stem	Root	Fruit	Seed	Leaf

3. In small groups, have students divide a sheet of lined paper into six columns and label each column with a plant part.
4. Challenge students to think of foods they eat that come from each plant part and record their answers on the lined paper.
5. Ask students to share their answers and record the lists on the chalkboard.

Flower	Fruit	Seed	Stem	Leaf	Root
cauliflower	tomato	peanuts	celery	lettuce	carrot
broccoli	plum	peas	asparagus	cabbage	radish
	apple				potato

Taking It Further . . .

Ask students to bring in pictures of different foods from magazines, newspapers, or grocery store circulars. Glue each picture on a 3" x 5" card to make a small set of playing cards. Students can use the cards for sorting games or play a game of concentration by matching pictures that represent the same plant part.

~• PLANT YOUR SOCKS •~

Materials:

- old, clean socks
- paper bags
- pots, aluminum trays, or pie tins (2" deep)
- potting soil

Lesson Procedure

1. Review how seeds travel as illustrated in *The Reason for a Flower*.
2. In the fall, plan a walking trip in a nearby field or wooded area where there are weeds and wildflowers.
3. Before the trip, ask each student to bring in one old cotton or wool sock that can be worn over a shoe. (Have a few extra socks from a thrift shop on hand for those students unable to bring one.)
4. On the day of the walk, ask students to put the old sock over one of their shoes. Don't tell them why. Keep it a mystery!
5. After students have walked around and explored the field or wooded area, ask them to remove the sock and carefully place it in a paper bag.
6. Back in the classroom, invite children to take a closer look at their socks to determine if they gathered any "hitchhikers." Discuss other ways plants disperse their seeds.
7. Encourage each student to place his or her sock in a tray or pie tin and cover it with potting soil.
8. Have students dampen the soil and the sock. Caution students not to over water.

Taking It Further . . .

After the plants begin to grow, students can try to identify the plants or conduct controlled experiments with varying amounts of water or light.

MYSTERY SEEDS

Materials:

- •worksheet on page 89
- •variety of seed packets
- •paper cups
- •potting soil
- •plastic sandwich bags
- •felt marker
- •masking tape

Lesson Procedure

1. Before beginning the lesson, check the amount of time needed for the different seeds to germinate—beans and radishes sprout in about three to four days. Remove the seeds from each packet and place them in a sandwich bag to make their identity a mystery.
2. Label each empty seed packet with a number and each sandwich bag with the corresponding number.
3. Give each group of four students a bag of "mystery" seeds and some potting soil.
4. Give each student a paper cup and invite students to plant the seeds in the containers. Using masking tape and a felt marker, label each container with the number on the sandwich bag.
5. Give each student a worksheet and invite students to fill in the top portion by describing their seeds and predicting what will grow.
6. Remind students to water the seeds over the next few days.
7. As the plants begin to sprout, remind students to measure growth and write new descriptions and predictions in their journals.
8. After the plants have grown large enough to identify, give students the original seed packets to verify their plant type.

Taking It Further . . .

Encourage students to write original poetry to describe their plants.

Name _____

Mystery Plant Journal

Planting date: _____

Describe your mystery-plant seeds.

_____

_____

What do you think will grow from your seeds?

_____

_____

Date: _____	Plant size: _____
Comments: _____	
_____	
Date: _____	Plant size: _____
Comments: _____	
_____	
Date: _____	Plant size: _____
Comments: _____	
_____	
Date: _____	Plant size: _____
Comments: _____	
_____	

The Ruth Heller Connection © 1992 Fearon Teacher Aids

❧• FICTIONAL FLOWERS •❧

Materials:

• *Designs for Coloring: Flowers* by Ruth Heller, 1985
• drawing paper
• pencils

Lesson Procedure

1. Challenge students to design their own imaginative flowers. Review the parts of a flower and explain that their "fictional flowers" should include these parts.

anther	stamen	stigma
style	stem	petal
sepal		

2. Encourage students to give their flowers a name and label the parts.
3. Students can get ideas from the coloring book, *Designs for Coloring: Flowers*.

Taking It Further . . .

Encourage students to write about the environment in which their fictional flowers grow. Be sure the students include an explanation for the specific reason for their flowers.

The Reason for a Flower

Materials:

- •assorted seeds (sunflower, peas, and peanuts)
- •paper cups
- •drawing paper
- •pencils

Lesson Procedure

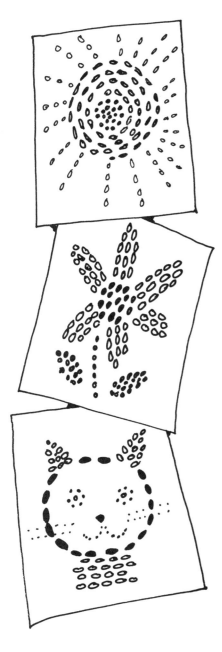

1. Give each student or group of students 3 to 4 cups with different seeds in each cup.
2. Write some math problems on the chalkboard.
3. Encourage students to use the seeds to solve the math problems.
4. Instruct students to write the math problems and answers on their papers as they solve them.

Taking It Further . . .

After students have computed the math problems, invite them to use the seeds, white glue, and heavy construction paper to create a mosaic.

MAY FLOWERS

Materials:

- construction paper
- scissors
- glue
- tape
- nut cups
- tissues
- string
- plastic straws or pipe cleaners

Lesson Procedure

1. Demonstrate how to make several kinds of paper flowers.

   Daffodils
   a. Cut petals from yellow construction paper.
   b. Glue the evenly spaced petals to the bottom of a nut cup.
   c. Add a straw stem and green paper leaves.

   Carnations
   a. Fold a tissue accordion-style and tie it in the center with string.
   b. Fluff the flower by gently pulling to separate the layers of tissue.
   c. Add a straw stem.

2. Invite students to make flowers.
3. Provide opportunities for students to experiment with the materials and encourage them to design other kinds of flowers as well.

Taking It Further . . .

Cover cardboard tissue rolls with gift wrap or contact paper to use as vases for the flowers.

Up, Up

Through imaginative text and lively illustrations, Ruth Heller embarks on another engaging journey into language. This time the destination is adverbs. Ms. Heller introduces words that tell how, how often, when, and where. Then she whisks the reader up, up and away into irregulars, superlatives, and double negatives.

ly

New York: Grosset & Dunlap, 1991

and Away

HOW DOES A PENGUIN DRESS?

Materials:

•worksheet on page 95
•pencils

Lesson Procedure

1. Discuss how adverbs explain how, how often, when, and where the action takes place.

   The grizzly growled *gruesomely.*
   The giraffe nibbles *gingerly.*
   Presently, he is jogging around the school.
   The twins live *there.*

2. Explain that many adverbs are made by adding -ly to adjectives.

   Our teacher is quick. She runs *quickly.*
   The dancer is dainty. She prances *daintily.*

3. Point out how Ruth Heller begins her book with "Penguins all dress decently." Challenge students to use the worksheet to list other adverbs describing how penguins might dress.

Taking It Further . . .

Share *Tacky the Penguin* by Helen Lester (Boston: Houghton Mifflin, 1988). Invite students to draw a penguin (or use the penguin on the worksheet), design a costume for it, and label it with an appropriate adverb.

Up, Up and Away

Name _____

How Does a Penguin Dress?

List as many adverbs as you can think of that describe how penguins might dress.

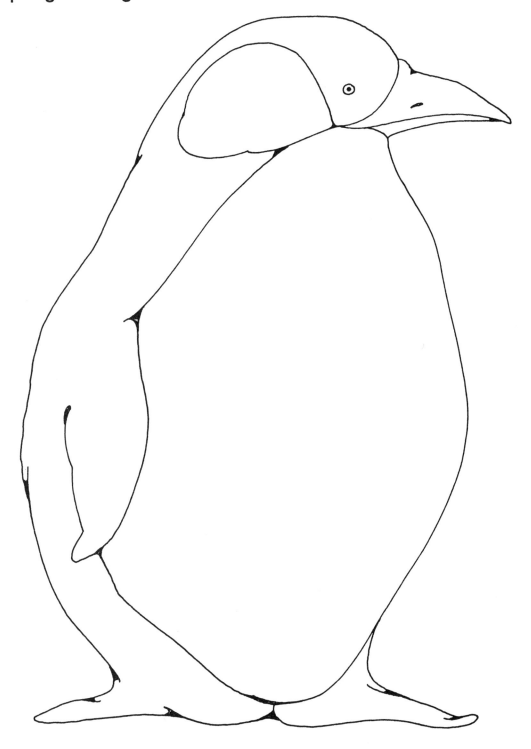

Up, Up and Away

SUPERLATIVE ACTION

Materials:

• lined paper
• pencils

Lesson Procedure

1. Review how comparative and superlative adjectives are formed by adding -er and -est. Explain how comparative and superlative adverbs are made the same way.

    Jan is fast. Jan runs fast.
    Louis is faster. Louis runs faster.
    Kris is the fastest. Kris runs the fastest.

2. Ask students to generate a list of animals and write the list on the chalkboard.
3. Ask students to generate a list of verbs and write the list on the chalkboard.
4. Challenge students to use the words from both lists to write sentences and then add comparative and superlative adverbs.

    The gorilla ran fast.
    The ostrich ran faster.
    The cheetah ran the fastest.

5. Remind students that adverbs ending in -ly can be used in comparative and superlative forms with *more* and *most, less* and *least.*

    The seal swims gracefully.
    The whale swims more gracefully.
    The shark swims most gracefully.

Taking It Further . . .

Write adverbs, such as slowly, fast, and haltingly, on 3" x 5" cards. Invite students to choose a card and act out the adverb. Classmates can guess the pantomimed word.